HOW TO
STOP BURNING
1 CRORE+PROFIT
WITH YOUR RICE HUSK

#1 Recommended Book for Paddy Business

HOW TO
STOP BURNING
1 CRORE+PROFIT
WITH YOUR RICE HUSK

#1 Recommended Book for Paddy Business

By

AMIT GARG

Worldwide Published by

Pendown Press

PENDOWN PRESS

An ISO 9001 & ISO 14001 certified Co.,

Regd. Office: 2525/193, 1st Floor, Onkar Nagar-A, Tri Nagar, Delhi-110035, (From Kanhaiya Nagar Metro Station Towards Old Bus Stand)

Branch Office: 1A/2A, 20, Hari Sadan, Ansari Road, Daryaganj, New Delhi-110002

Ph.: 09350849407, 011-27387998

E-mail: info@pendownpress.com

Website: PendownPress.com

First Edition: 2020

Price: ₹259/-

ISBN: 978-93-89601-75-6

Layout and Cover Designed by Pendown Graphics Team

Printed and Bound in India by Thomson Press India Ltd.

CONTENT

List

ABOUT ME

Hello, I am Amit Garg. I am science graduate and have done MASTERS from Indian Rubber Manufacturers Association. I am the director of one of the leading firms in the rubber industry.

My mission is to make my company world's top manufacturer of rice rubber rollers and also the whitener stones being used to polish the rice. I have tried my level best to use my technical background to make one of the finest qualities of PHENOL FORMALDEHYDE RESINS in the world and hence the RUBBER ROLL.

1

REASONS FOR THE EXPANSION OF RICE MILL INDUSTRY

Today, many new companies are making an entry into the highly competitive rice mill industry. More and more businesses can be seen setting up millions of rupees worth of rice plants in different parts of India.

The reason behind such quick expansion is two-fold:

1. To gain better value for their investments since better quality rice always yields a better price in the market.

> *There cannot be a stronger natural right*
> *than that of a man's making the best profit he*
> *can of the natural produce of his lands.*
>
> *–Benjamin Franklin*

2. Achieve higher productivity that will lower the fixed capital and labour costs while increasing the TOPLINE of the company.

RICE RUBBER ROLLS AND THE HINDUSTAN GROUP

The Hindustan Group has been a major player in the rice rubber roll industry for the past 35 years. We pride ourselves for our capacity to manufacture 1,400 rice rubber rolls per day.

DID YOU KNOW?

Many ingredients are used to make rubber compound of rice rollers, and this includes PHENOL FORMALDEHYDE RESIN.

2

THE ROLE OF PHENOL FORMALDEHYDE RESIN (P.F. RESIN)

The reason for adding Phenol Formaldehyde Resin to the rubber roll compound is primarily to increase its modulus or the force that is required to stretch a given compound to double its length.

If a compound is low in hardness, it will apply a lower force as compared to a harder compound.

> *Profit in business comes from repeat customers, customers that boast about your project or service, and that bring friends with them.*
>
> *—W. Edwards Deming*

To remove the husk from paddy, a higher modulus product is required. It means that even if we make the compound with all the excellent properties such as tensile strength, elongation at break and abrasion, but if the modulus is lower, it won't be able to remove the husk.

P. F. RESIN has a crucial role in the manufacturing of rice rubber rolls.

3

MAKING OF NEW AGE RUBBER ROLL 2.0 BY P. F. RESIN

P. F. RESIN has a very low shelf life. After just one week of making a fresh batch, one of its key properties which is, Norton's flow, begins to diminish.

This is where the HINDUSTAN GROUP comes up with a winning solution and makes its presence felt!

We are the only company on this planet that has set-up a separate plant to manufacture this highly sought-after component, P.F. Resin.

Our specialized plant by the name BIMEL RESINS PVT LTD. gives us the control to manufacture rubber rolls with an exceptional modulus that has an excellent shelf life with minimum breakage of rice.

We call this revolutionary product – THE HINDUSTAN GROUP'S NEW AGE RUBBER ROLLS 2.0

4

THE SUCCESSFUL DISCOVERY

When it comes to Raw or Steam Rice, the general practice, for as long as one can remember, has always been to use rubber rolls with a lower hardness, the aim being to reduce the percentage of broken rice. However, one major drawback or side effect of this practice was a lesser roll-life.

In the case of Parboiled Rice, people were using rubber rolls with a higher level of hardness which had a higher roll-life but had to compromise on a slightly higher percentage of broken rice.

After receiving feedback from several overseas as well as Indian customers, and after several, yet failed attempts, the Hindustan Group was finally able to create rubber rolls which can be used on Raw as well as Parboiled rice with the same hardness and quality.

5

TOP FEATURES & RESULTING BENEFITS OF OUR NEW AGE RUBBER ROLLS 2.0

- HIGH OUTPUT: An output as high as 500 MT (Parboiled Paddy) and 300 MT (Raw Paddy)

- SMOOTH FUNCTIONING: Advanced compounding of rolls leading to exceptionally smooth functioning.

- HIGH SHELLING EFFICIENCY: Soundless and vibration-free running of rolls.

- LOWER PERCENTAGE OF BROKEN RICE: Huge savings in costs due to lower broken rice.

COST CUTTING

In most 10" rice rubber rolls, the base of the roll is a metal core made of Aluminium. In case the base is not good, the roll will never be able to produce the desired results.

To control the costs and to get the Aluminium drums with the best required consistent parameters, we have set up a PRESSURE DIE CASTING unit to make Aluminium drums by using ADC 12 alloy. After this process, the shell is given the exact size and shape by turning on the CNC machine.

6

OUR SUCCESS STORY

A CASE STUDY OF MR. ARIF MOHAMMAD BY HINDUSTAN GROUP

During one of my yearly visits to Bangladesh to meet an old client, I requested him to give me a reference. My client obliged and gave me the reference to one of his dear friends, Mr. Arif Mohammad.

THE CHALLENGE

On meeting Mr. Arif, I discovered that he was going through a rough patch. Since I was a reference from his dear friend, Mr. Arif readily discussed the various problems he had been facing. He told me that he had set up a 15 MT per hour capacity BUHLER plant but he was unable to fulfill even his interest liability.

> *A person is born with a liking for profit.*
>
> *—Xun Kuang*

THE SOLUTION

- After understanding his situation, here are some of the changes I suggested to him, on behalf of the HINDUSTAN GROUP:

- Change the Rubber Roll and Whitener Stone.

- Upgrade Your Staff. The previous head of production had a little knowledge about how to run the plant. The only USP that he had was his social networking skills and was more concerned about building his clientage.

THE ADDED BENEFIT

- I also introduced Mr. Arif to a person who was looking for a job and had good day-to-day experience in running a plant.

THE RESULTS

- Today, Mr. Arif is in the process of setting up his brand-new plant and has also become our family friend.

- The small changes that we had suggested for his plant have shown wonderful results:

- Mr. Arif is now producing more white and shining rice, and thus, getting a greater value for his rice.

- The final broken percentage of rice is down by approximately 1.2%, leading to huge yearly savings.

- His plant now runs for an average 21 hours per day instead of the previous 18 hours leading to decreased costs and more volumes of rice at the same fixed capital and labour costs. There are also far lesser breakdowns due to silky smooth running of machines.

We, in the Hindustan Group, are committed to our clients' success and leave no stones unturned in making a widespread contribution to their growth and value addition.

We are quite sure that our revolutionary New Age Rice Rolls 2.0 will change the face of the paddy industry by cutting down on wastages and save rice mill owners crores of rupees.

Notes: